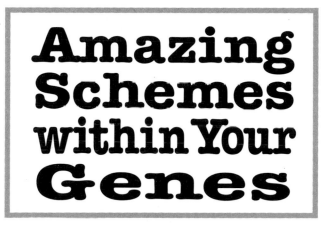

Amazing Schemes within Your Genes

by Dr. Fran [ces R.] Balkwill
illustrated by Mic Rolph

Carolrhoda Books, Inc./Minneapolis

This edition first published 1993 by Carolrhoda Books, Inc.

Library of Congress Cataloging-in-Publication Data

Balkwill, Frances R.
    Amazing schemes within your genes / by Fran Balkwill ; illustrated by Mic Rolph.
        p.   cm.
    Summary: Discusses the structure and function of genes, their adaptations and mutations, and basic genetic processes, particularly as they occur in humans.
    ISBN 0-87614-804-6
    1. Genes – Juvenile literature. 2. Human genetics – Juvenile literature. [1. Genetics.] I. Rolph, Mic, ill. II. Title. III. Series.
QH447.B35   1993
573.2'1 – dc20   92-42942
                                                                      CIP
                                                                       AC

Manufactured in the United States of America

1 2 3 4 5 6 98 97 96 95 94 93

Think of all the people you know and see every day. Your family, your friends, people who live or work in your neighborhood – even people on the radio and television. Then think of all the people who live in villages, towns, and cities throughout your country. Try to imagine all the millions and millions of people who live in villages, towns, and cities around the world. There are more than five billion children, men, and women sharing the planet with you. If you could line them all up, the line would stretch from the earth to the moon – and back again – six times! And the amazing fact is . . .

. . . not *one* of those five billion other people looks, thinks, or behaves exactly like you! You are completely unique.

Why is that?

Well, to make you the way you are, there are some amazing schemes within your genes.

So what are genes?

5

Genes are recipes for making proteins, which are important substances in your body. Proteins make the cells in your body the shape and color they are. Proteins help cells do all the complicated jobs they have to do. You have about fifty thousand genes inside you. There are genes for the many different proteins that make your eyes, ears, nose, and mouth; genes for proteins that make your fingernails and toenails, your teeth and hair; genes for proteins that make your brain, lungs, and heart; genes for proteins that influence your height, your senses of taste and smell, and even genes for proteins that decide your skin and hair color.

Where exactly do you find genes?

Errr!...

Your genes are in each of the hundred million million cells in your body.

Your cells are making new cells all the time. This skin cell is about to divide into two. If you look closely, you can see dark shapes in the center of the dividing cell. These shapes are called **chromosomes** (KRO-muh-sohmz). Each of your cells has 46 chromosomes – 23 pairs – inside it.

If you could unravel one chromosome from one of your cells and look at it under a mega-powerful electron microscope, you would find that chromosomes are made of a threadlike substance called deoxyribonucleic (dee-ahk-see-ry-boh-noo-KLEE-ik) acid, or **DNA** for short.

Genes are made of this DNA.

If each gene is a recipe, then DNA is the chemical language that the recipes are written in. There are gene recipes all along the DNA threads that are wound up in each chromosome. All gene recipes are made from just four different chemicals joined to each other along the DNA strand. These chemicals are:

Adenine (AD-uh-neen)
Thymine (THY-meen)
Cytosine (SYT-uh-seen)
Guanine (GWAHN-een)

Scientists call them **A, T, C,** and **G.** We've drawn each one in a different color.

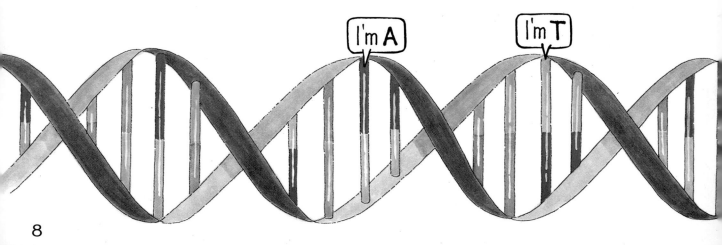

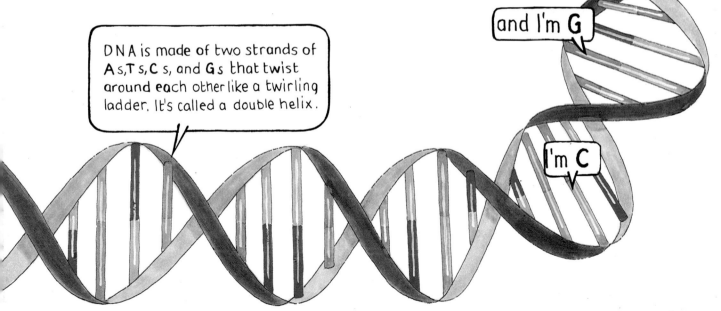

Not all of your DNA makes gene recipes. Along each chromosome there are long stretches of DNA with no meaning at all, just endless repeats, such as **CGCGCGCGCGCGCGCGCGCGCGCGCGCGCGCG.** But then the sequence changes, and you find a gene. Each gene has several thousand **A**s, **T**s, **C**s, and **G**s joined together in a precise code that is different from the code for any other gene.

Every second of every minute of every hour, your cells are using gene recipes to make the proteins they need.

How do cells make proteins?

DNA is made of two strands of As,Ts,Cs, and Gs that twist around each other like a twirling ladder. It's called a double helix.

and I'm G

I'm C

1. When a protein is needed, the part of the DNA that is the gene for that protein unwinds from its chromosome.

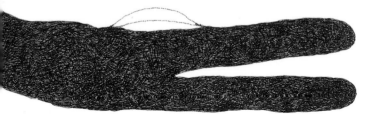

2. Then a copy of the gene is made from one of the two DNA strands.

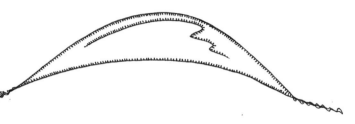

3. The copy strand floats off to another part of the cell, the **ribosome.** Here it acts as a pattern for building a protein.

Here I go!!

RIBOSOME

4. Proteins are assembled from building blocks called **amino acids** that float around inside the cell.

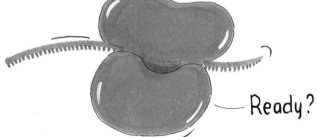

Ready?

5. The copy strand tells the cell the correct order for the amino acids, which join up like the beads on a very long necklace. The necklace of amino acids then folds up tightly. The shape is different for each protein.

PROTEIN

Yipeeee!!

So, as you read this book, remember that:

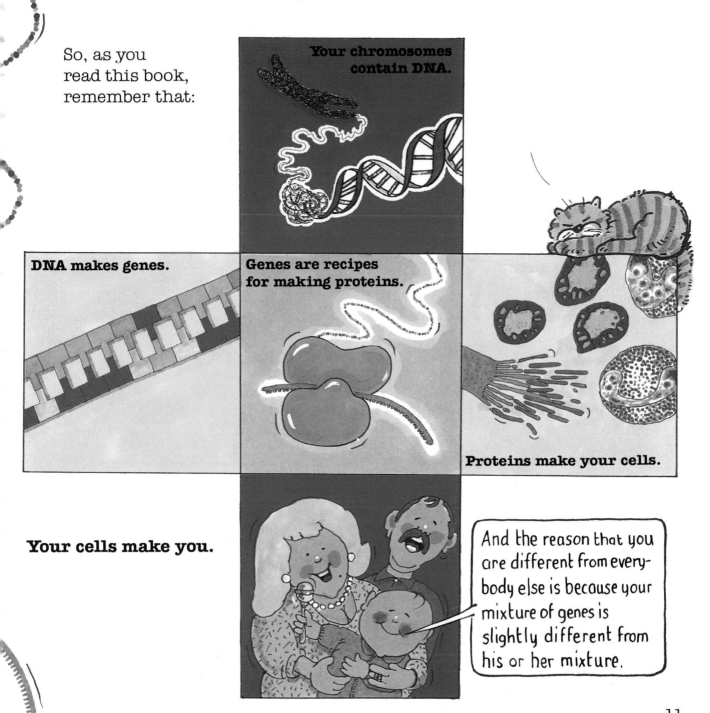

Your chromosomes contain DNA.

DNA makes genes.

Genes are recipes for making proteins.

Proteins make your cells.

Your cells make you.

And the reason that you are different from everybody else is because your mixture of genes is slightly different from his or her mixture.

How did you get your unique mixture of genes? You were created when two cells fused together – one cell from your father (the sperm) and one from your mother (the egg). Sperm and egg cells are made in a special way. They don't have 23 pairs of chromosomes like all the other cells in your body – they each have only 23 single chromosomes.

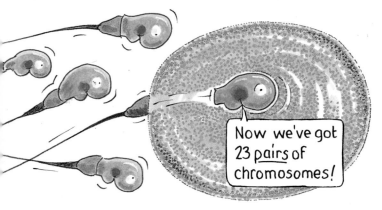

Now we've got 23 pairs of chromosomes!

When the sperm and the egg join together, the first cell of the new human being has 23 pairs of chromosomes again, 23 from the egg and 23 from the sperm. So your 46 chromosomes are a mixture of your parents' chromosomes, and your genes are a mixture of their genes. But your mixture of genes is different from that of both of your parents. Why?

This is the really amazing part.

When the sperm or eggs are being made, each pair of chromosomes interlocks, and genes are swapped from one chromosome in each pair to the other. So each individual egg or sperm contains a mixture of genes that is completely original – different from every other egg or sperm.

I didn't know that!

Here's how it works.

Let's look at just one pair of chromosomes.

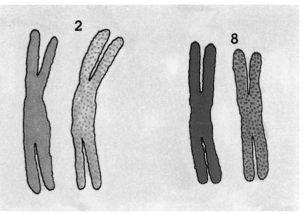

1. The chromosomes have made copies of their DNA and now become shorter and thicker. They move very close to their copies.

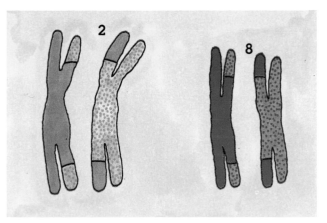

3. When the chromosome pairs part, they have exchanged some of their DNA. Each has a different mixture of genes from the original pair.

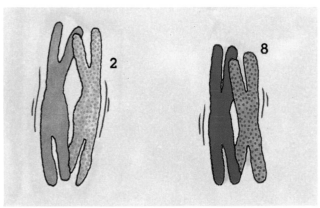

2. The "arms" of the chromosomes coil around each other. They can stay like this for a very long time. All eggs, for instance, reach this stage before a girl is born, and the arms don't uncoil from each other until the girl matures, 10 to 15 years later.

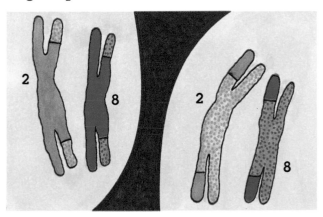

4. But the egg and sperm cells still have 23 pairs of chromosomes. What happens next? The cell divides again, but this time one chromosome from each pair goes into each cell. **The egg and sperm are finally ready to make a new human being!**

He's about to find out
the difference between
boys and girls!!

When you started your life, you were
made of just one tiny cell with 23
pairs of chromosomes containing a
unique mixture of genes. But now that
same mixture of genes is in the millions

**CRINGE
SWEAT/
GULP.**

and millions of cells that make up your body.
How does this happen? Well, you grew because
that first cell became two cells, those two
cells became four, four became eight, and
so on, until you were made of millions of cells.
Before each cell divided, the DNA that makes
your genes was copied so that each new cell
would contain your genes as well.

How do genes make the difference between this girl and boy?

Just one gene on one special
chromosome makes the difference!
If we take a cell from each child and
look through a microscope at their
chromosomes, we can pick out the 23
pairs – in the girl. But we can only
make out 22 pairs in the boy. What
about the other pair? The
chromosomes
don't look alike!
One is shaped
like an **X,** and the
other is smaller
and looks like
an upside-down **Y.**

life line

protect the rainforests

14

All human embryos start developing in the same way. But if the embryo has two **X** chromosomes, an area of cells becomes the egg-making part (the ovaries), and the baby will be a girl. If the embryo has a **Y** chromosome, a protein made from one gene on the **Y** chromosome signals some of the cells to start forming the sperm-making part (the testes). Once this has happened, the baby will be a boy. Many more genes then make many more proteins that cause the differences that you can see between girls and boys. But without that one gene on the **Y** chromosome, we would all be girls.

Just imagine.

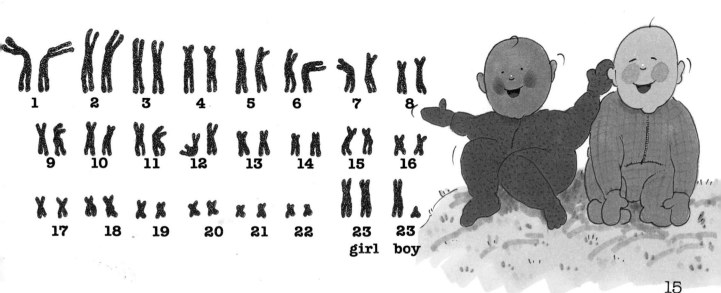

1   2   3   4   5   6   7   8

9   10   11   12   13   14   15   16

17   18   19   20   21   22   23   23
                                    girl   boy

Of course, human beings are different from each other in many, many ways. It is not always easy to understand the influence of genes on these differences, but there are some very obvious clues. Take a good look at all the families you know and see if you can find some of these inherited features. Now there is no need to be bored at large family gatherings – you can play the genetic detective! See if you can spot other inherited differences, and guess who is related to whom.

Occasionally you can find very strong evidence for one particular pattern of inheritance. (For example, look for a family in which both parents have red hair.) But most patterns of inheritance are not so simple. Most differences between human beings – height and skin color, for example – are controlled by more than one gene. Another reason that patterns of inheritance are complicated is that we all have *two* copies of every gene on each pair of chromosomes, one each from our fathers and mothers. Both copies can be used by your cells.

And you must remember that the way you live, the food you eat, and all the many experiences you have act on the raw material of your genes to help make you the way you are.

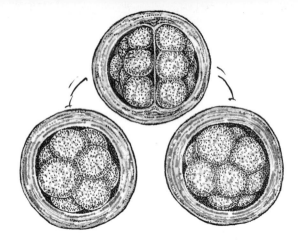

Is it really true that *every* human being is unique? What about twins? Do you know any? Maybe you are one! There are two types of twins, identical and fraternal. Identical twins have identical genes. Sometimes during the first two weeks of life, the tiny ball of cells that is a new human being splits into two. From that point on, two babies begin to develop. After they are born, sometimes even their mother can't tell them apart!

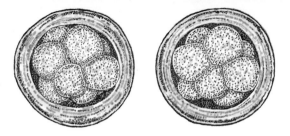

Identical twins are the same sex, they have the same color eyes, and the shapes of their noses and ears are identical. Even if identical twins are separated at birth and raised in different families, they can turn out to be remarkably alike.

But not all twins have identical genes. Fraternal twins are made when the mother produces two eggs at the same time. So two sperm fuse with two eggs to make two babies with very different mixtures of genes. These twins are no more like each other than other brothers and sisters, except that they share a birthday.

You may know someone who is an electrical engineer, or a mechanical engineer, or even a chemical engineer, but have you ever heard of a genetic engineer? There are thousands of them in the world today, and the experiments they are doing now will undoubtedly affect your life as you grow up. Can you imagine, for instance, that genetic engineers can take human genes – each just a tiny fraction of a millimeter in size – and put them into bacteria?

20

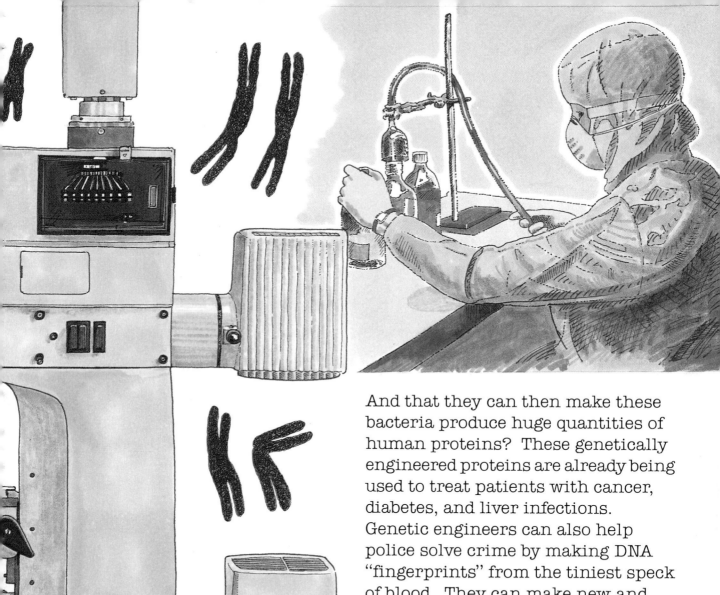

And that they can then make these bacteria produce huge quantities of human proteins? These genetically engineered proteins are already being used to treat patients with cancer, diabetes, and liver infections. Genetic engineers can also help police solve crime by making DNA "fingerprints" from the tiniest speck of blood. They can make new and better medicines to protect us against serious diseases, and in the near future, they may be able to cure people who have faulty genes.

We've already told you that every time one of your cells divides into two, a copy is made of all your genes. A faulty gene is produced when a mistake is made by a cell as it copies a gene, or when DNA is damaged. Mistakes in genes are called **mutations** (myoo-TAY-shunz) – and they take place all the time. Cells with a mutant (faulty) gene may not do their jobs properly, but you have one hundred million million cells in your body. Most cells with faulty genes will soon die and be replaced by healthy ones.

Can you spot the difference?

But what happens if there are mutations in the genes of sperm or egg cells? If sperm or egg cells with faulty genes do not die, they may make new human beings. In this way, mutations can be passed on to the next generation. Some inherited mutations don't cause much trouble. For instance, color blindness is not a very serious condition...

Can you see the shapes inside the circles? If you can't, you have probably inherited color blindness. Most people can see three basic colors – red, blue, and green. This allows them to see all the different colors in our world. But some children inherit a mutation in one of the genes for an eye cell protein. Their eye cells don't work in the usual way. Most people who have color blindness cannot tell the difference between red and green (which can make it difficult to know when to cross the street!). Some color-blind people confuse blue and yellow. A very few people are totally color blind, and their world is nothing but shades of gray.

Here's another job for the genetic detective – do our color test on all your friends, classmates, and relatives.

If you test enough children, you may notice that most children with color blindness are boys.
    Do you know why?

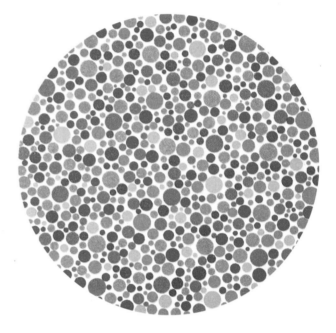

Clue: The faulty gene is on the **X** chromosome. You may remember that the **Y** chromosome is smaller than the **X**. Because of this, boys have only one copy of many of the genes found on the **X** chromosome. A girl may have a faulty gene for the eye cell protein on one of her **X** chromosomes. But if the same gene on her second **X** chromosome is healthy, she won't be color-blind. Boys, on the other hand, have only one chance at having a healthy copy of the gene.

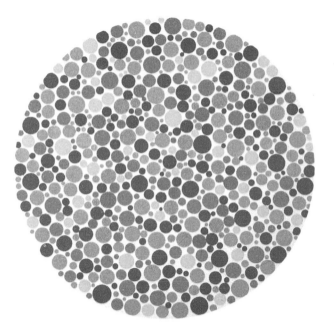
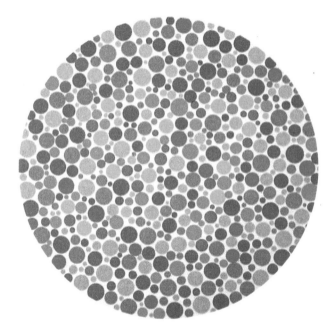

Other inherited mutations are more serious and can make people ill. There are over five thousand human diseases that are caused by inherited mutations in our genes.

One of these diseases is called cystic fibrosis (SIS-tik fy-BRO-sis). Children with this illness have one faulty gene. This gene makes a protein that normally helps the cells that line the lungs and digestive system keep the tubes clear, moist, and full of sticky mucus to trap germs. Because of this faulty protein, the lungs of children with cystic fibrosis become clogged with extra thick mucus. This can make it difficult for people with cystic fibrosis to breathe. Bacteria grow in the lungs and make the children ill. Parts of their digestive systems become blocked, and they can't digest their food properly. Nowadays nurses and doctors use treatments to keep children with cystic fibrosis healthy and help them lead better lives, though the disease cannot be cured. In the future, genetic engineers may be able to replace the faulty gene and make the children better.

Scientists have discovered that the faulty gene for cystic fibrosis is on chromosome 7.

affected

How do children get cystic fibrosis? In North America, Britain, and northern Europe, about 1 person in 25 has one faulty gene and one normal gene for this protein. They are perfectly healthy, because the one correct gene makes all the correct proteins their cells need. But if a mother and a father each have one faulty gene, some of their children could inherit two faulty genes. Those children will be born with cystic fibrosis.

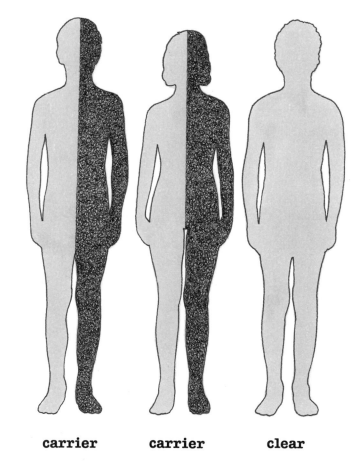

father
carrier

mother
carrier

carrier

carrier

clear

Millions of people in the world suffer from
sickle-cell anemia (uh-NEE-mee-uh).
This disease is caused by a mutation in
the gene for hemoglobin (HEE-muh-
gloh-bin). Hemoglobin is the protein
in red blood cells that carries oxygen
from your lungs to the rest of your body.
Red blood cells are normally round and
smooth, but some red blood cells in
children with sickle-cell anemia are long,
curved, and thin – like sickles – because
the faulty hemoglobin does not keep
them the right shape. Sickle cells block
up tiny blood vessels and don't live as
long as normal red cells. This means
that children with the disease often
become tired and ill, and are in pain.
Nowadays doctors and nurses have many
ways to help these children.

Like children with cystic fibrosis,
children with sickle-cell anemia have
two copies of the faulty gene – one
inherited from each of their parents.
One in 10 people who live in, or have
ancestors who come from, Africa or the
Caribbean region, have one normal and
one faulty gene for hemoglobin. This
disease is also found among people from
the Middle East, the Mediterranean
region, and Asia.

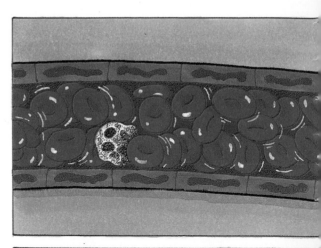

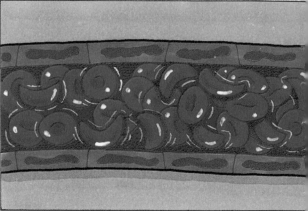

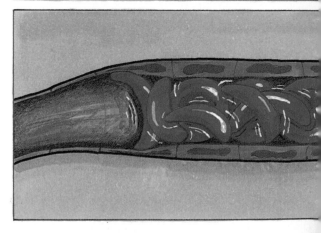

How did sickle-cell anemia start?

About ten thousand years ago, when some early human beings lived in hot and humid regions of the world, a deadly disease developed. We now call that disease malaria (muh-LAIR-ee-uh). The malaria germ grew in the livers and red blood cells of humans. It was easily spread by mosquitoes who bit infected people. Malaria made people feverish and weak. Many of them died. But after several hundred years, there were a few people who didn't get malaria, or didn't get such bad cases of it. This was because a mutation had taken place in one of the hemoglobin genes. Although these people, with one normal and one faulty gene for hemoglobin, were healthy, their red blood cells had changed slightly, and the malaria germ couldn't grow in them. Thousands of years passed. People with one faulty hemoglobin gene lived longer than others because they were resistant to malaria. So these people had more children, who also inherited the faulty gene. Soon children were born to parents who each had one faulty gene. Some of their children inherited two copies of the faulty gene and were born with sickle-cell anemia.

GLUG!!

Although mutations can be bad, they can be useful as well. All forms of life on this planet have genes made of DNA in their cells. Mutations allow living creatures to change in order to get used to new surroundings. Mutations create new species. Mutations are the reason that life on earth has developed from a single-celled ancestor into millions of different plants and animals. Take you, for instance. You are a member of the species *Homo sapiens.* Your closest living relatives are the apes. In fact, 98.4 percent of your genes are the same as the genes of any chimpanzee you might see in a wildlife park or zoo.

About twenty million years ago, your ancestors lived in tropical woodlands. Their bodies were well suited to climbing trees, and they lived and hunted in groups. Three or four million years ago, useful mutations happened so that some of your ancestors were able to walk upright on two legs. The shape of the bones in their hips, knees, and feet changed, and their arms became shorter than their legs. Then they could travel farther to find food and move faster to escape hungry predators. Their hands, freed from helping them move along the ground, developed a powerful, precise grip. Between one and two million years ago, more useful mutations gave these apes larger brains.

Then they invented many tools from the wood and stone around them. They began to communicate and help each other hunt for food.

Just forty thousand years ago, the first true members of our species began to populate the planet.

Scientists studying our genes now know that we are
all descended from that small group of early humans.
Whether our skins and hair are light or dark, whether
we now live in the Arctic or at the equator, the message
of our genes tells us that we are brothers and sisters...